handing on the faith

Other ***Handing on the Faith*** titles:

When You Are a Catechist

When You Are a Confirmation Sponsor

When You Are a Godparent

When You Are a Grandparent

When You Are an RCIA Sponsor

Your Child's Baptism

Your Child's Confirmation

Your Child's First Communion

Your Child's First Penance

To the Many Parents, Pastors and Spiritual Directors
whose words of insight and wisdom,
often gained through painful experience,
are contained here,
my sincerest gratitude.

When Your
Adult Child Chooses
a Different Path

Theresa Cotter

ST. ANTHONY MESSENGER PRESS
Cincinnati, Ohio

Scripture citations are taken from The *New Revised Standard Version Bible*, copyright
©1989 by the Division of Christian Education of the National Council of the Churches
of Christ in the United States of America, and used by permission. All rights reserved.

Excerpts from Bill Huebsch's *Vatican II in Plain English: The Decrees and Declarations,
Book 3,* copyright © 1997, are used by permission of Thomas More Publishing.

Cover and interior illustrations by Julie Lonneman
Cover and book design by Mary Alfieri

Library of Congress Cataloging-in-Publication Data

Cotter, Theresa.
  When your adult child chooses a different path / Theresa Cotter.
     p. cm. — (Handing on the faith)
  ISBN 0-86716-484-0 (pbk.)
  1. Parenting—Religious aspects—Catholic Church. 2. Adult
children—Religious life. I. Title. II. Series.
  BX2352 .C68 2002
  248.8'45—dc21

                                    2002002147

ISBN 0-86716-484-0

Published by St. Anthony Messenger Press
www.AmericanCatholic.org
Printed in the U.S.A.

Contents

Introduction

Is there anyone more idealistic than the parents of a newborn? We looked at that baby in endless fascination, overcome with awe and with fear: awe at the mystery of life and this creation that we held in our hands and fear of the responsibility for raising this child to adulthood. At some point in this mixture of emotion we promised to that child and to ourselves that we would be perfect—or near perfect—parents, for this newborn babe deserved nothing less.

We were determined to pass on to this child all the values that are most important to us, including our Catholic faith. Then, we believed in all innocence and ignorance, when our child reached adulthood our parenting responsibilities would be completed, we would reap our just rewards and, with humble gratitude, receive the honor and adulation of family and friends.

But then, as one parent described it, "Life banged us up against mystery." We learned very soon of our own imperfections and limitations and of the definite personality of our child. Now, instead of the realization of our dreams, we are confronted with crisis. Despite our efforts and our waiting times of faith, despite years of words and example and prayers, we are in a situation that we never envisioned. The details vary: We have a son who has married into another Christian denomination. Our daughter is pregnant and not married. Our son is living a materialistic, no-time-for-religion lifestyle. Our daughter has become a Jew (or Buddhist or Muslim or...). Our son has "come out" and is in a gay relationship. Our daughter is getting another divorce. Our son is into drugs and has severed all ties with our family. The list of possibilities seems endless. We are heartbroken. We feel both guilty and betrayed. Our pain is deep.

We struggle with knowing how to respond. How do we sustain a relationship with our child? Or should we?

Letting Go

When we parents are confronted with an adult child who decides to go in a different direction, we are often glibly told, "Let go!"

But let go of what? The relationship? Dreams? Guilt? Love? Embarrassment? The desire to be friends with our child? Anger? Feelings of failure? Disappointment? Our values? Communication? The pain? Our integrity? The memories? Our hopes? Resentment? Everything?

Having survived our child's adolescence, we know how little control we have over our adult offspring. While we may harbor a remnant of desire for control, most of us are quite ready to enter into an adult relationship with this person in whom we've invested so much. We cannot erase the joy-filled memories. Dreams do persist. The longing for a close relationship remains. Hope and love continue beyond all reason. As Saint Paul reminds us, "Love never ends" (1 Corinthians 13:8). That is true of God's love for us and our love for our child.

So what about "letting go"?

Desire to control may linger out of habit, for we've

had responsibility for this child for many years. Letting go of control is not difficult when our adult child is mature, well established in a profession, married to someone of whom we approve, faithfully practices the Catholic faith, lives an approved lifestyle and still finds time to honor us appropriately.

Letting go of control when the situation is, according to our expectations, not acceptable, is another matter. We wonder, is this our last opportunity to influence our child? If we don't control our child's behavior, will we lose both the child and the relationship? Are we responding out of guilt or resentment or parental pride? Is it possible that we need to maintain control because, deep down, we really don't believe in God?

Unfortunately, just feeling that we must be in the director's chair may contribute to the problem!

▶ Some parents can't give up control easily, just as some people direct traffic no matter where they are. (A parent and spiritual director)

▶ God works in mysterious ways—but God works! (A parent)

▶ Let go—but maintain engagement. (A parent and spiritual director)

▶ There comes a time when children are fledged! (A parent who is a birder and spiritual director)

Intellectually we know that parenting is the vocation of weaning a child to independence—physical, psychological, spiritual. However, there also comes a time when we need to wean ourselves, not only from our desire to control but also from feelings of responsibility, from guilt and embarrassment, from resentment and anger. We did the best we could with what we had at the time. We love our child and we have always wanted to be good parents—we were and still are! So we are not to let go of parenting, which has merely shifted into another phase, this one as important as all the preceding phases. Our parenting continues through the example of our actions: To our child we remain the prime example of love, of faith in God and the guidance of the Holy Spirit. In addition, we set the tone for how others respond to situations, for siblings and friends and the extended family often take their cue from us.

As we have taught Christianity, so we are now to be Christianity toward our own child. As we have taught acceptance and respect for all people, so we are now to accept and respect our child and that child's decisions and lifestyle. As we have taught God's all-embracing love and mercy, so we are now to embody that love and mercy toward our own child. Pope John XXIII said, "Remember that Christ's eighth sacrament is you."

We are to let go of control, of resentment and anger and pain and, yes, even of dreams and goals that are ours but not our child's. None of us is to be held rigid by the bonds of either memory or wishful daydreaming, no matter how loving those bonds or praiseworthy those dreams.

Some people perceive letting go as passive and weak behavior, an admission of defeat. They've never tried it!

Often we do not let go until we have exhausted all other actions and in absolute desperation cry out, "I surrender! I don't know what else to do. I give my child back to you, God!" We are not mouthing the words—it is a wrenching heart cry emanating from our core being. In that exact instant, even though the situation has not changed, *we* have!

In letting go, we are eloquently enumerating our beliefs: We are recognizing that God is active in all our lives. We are affirming our child as a unique creature of God who is directed by the Holy Spirit. We are making an act of absolute faith and trust in God. We are moving from the parent/child relationship to an adult/adult relationship. We are opening ourselves to the inspiration of the Holy Spirit and to continued learning and growing. We are admitting that, while we don't understand God's ways, we do believe in the miraculous working power of the Divine.

Paradoxically, letting go of control, of feelings of guilt and responsibility and regret, can be the most positive action available. We are affirming that we are no longer responsible for our child's actions. Letting go of our dreams and parental goals makes room for our child's dreams and life goals. Letting go creates space for relationships to change and mature. Letting go allows us to cast off negative thought patterns, becoming open to new and creative ways of relating, imaginative ways of loving.

Our Fears

A spiritual director I know says, "When a parent comes to me, concerned about an apparently wayward adult child, my first question is, 'What do you, the parent, fear?'"

A good starting point in any quandary is to ask ourselves, "What do I fear? What is my deepest concern?"

When I was very young the good nuns told me that only Catholics could get to heaven. While I don't believe that any more, the echoes of that statement remain in my mind—especially now, since one of the non-Catholics is my son. (A parent)

Such memories and rumors and handed-down sayings continue to haunt us, like ghosts delighting to appear when we are most fragile and vulnerable. Thankfully, the church has officially corrected such distorted theology— theology that painted an insultingly unloving picture of God. As the Second Vatican Council assured us, God wills the salvation of everyone!

God is not the avenging judge, the meticulous record-keeper, the harsh disciplinarian. God judges and disciplines with mercy and loving-kindness. God does not and will not abandon us or our children. God is love—inclusive, radical love. When we wander astray, God never forbids our return. When our child wanders astray, God never forbids that child's return but instead promises an open welcome.

Of course we are all God's children, each of us loved more than we can possibly comprehend. Of course God is bigger than any one church or group or religion. Of course someone can be saved even if that person does not know Christ or his church.

The Second Vatican Council hereby declares that human beings have a right to religious liberty. This means that no one is to be forced by other individuals, by social groups, or by any other human power regarding religious matters. No one should ever be forced to act in a way that is contrary to his or her beliefs. Nor should anyone ever be kept from acting according to those beliefs, whether in private or in public, alone or in a social group, within appropriate limits. This right is rooted in the nature of what it means to be human; it is founded in human dignity, which is made known to us both through the revealed Word and by reason. (*Dignitatis Humanae* ["Declaration on Religious Freedom"], from Bill Huebsch, *Vatican II in Plain English: The Decrees and Declarations, Book 3* [Allen, Tex.: Thomas More Publishing, 1997], p. 73)

And, of course we continue to pray, praying prayers that reflect this theology of love. We pray that our daughter has the courage to be open to the wisdom of the Holy Spirit. We pray that our son is sensitive to God's call, whatever that call may be. We pray that we ourselves are liberated from the fears that rule our narrowness of thought, for faith is broader than religion.

Our fears may also be of matters quite practical. We may fear that our empty nest will be called upon to house grown children and energetic grandchildren. We may fear for the physical safety of our gay son. We may fear that this latest crisis will cause deep divisions within the family. We may fear for the financial security of the family.

▶ When our handicapped son was born years ago I worried whether I would be able to love him. Now I know how very much I do love him. If I, a mere human being, can love a retarded child, I no longer have any doubts about our Creator's love for each and every one of us. (A parent)

▶ Our son has rejected us, his family. I see the relationship that other parents have with their children and I want it, too! (A Lutheran pastor and parent)

These matters do indeed need to be addressed. We turn to the Serenity Prayer to help us determine what is under our control and what is not—and then tend to those matters we can, relying on available resources and assistance. We do not hesitate to call on others for help, for that is community. The rest of our fears we place in God's hands.

SERENITY PRAYER

GOD grant me the serenity
to accept the things
I cannot change,

Courage to change the
things I can, and the
wisdom to know the difference.

Another common fear is the loss of a dream. All people have hopes and dreams of the future, but parents have them in abundance. Raising a child is an act of faith into the forever-future. This faith comes accompanied with wonderful, joy-filled, laudable dreams of what is to come! Our dreams provide goals and consolation, sustaining us through both the difficult times and the dailyness of parenting.

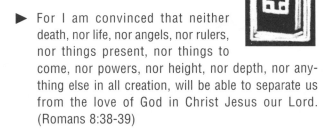

▶ For I am convinced that neither death, nor life, nor angels, nor rulers, nor things present, nor things to come, nor powers, nor height, nor depth, nor anything else in all creation, will be able to separate us from the love of God in Christ Jesus our Lord. (Romans 8:38-39)

▶ ...The LORD is my rock, my fortress, and my deliverer, my God, my rock in whom I take refuge, my shield, and the horn of my salvation, my stronghold. (Psalms 18:2)

We have dreams that affirm us as good, dedicated parents: our child following in the family business, our child's children united with us in the practice of our Catholic faith, our child a close and loving friend, our child ordained or in the religious life, our family as our solace in old age.

Unfortunately, dreams can also become roadblocks in the unfolding of our child's personality and talents, especially when the very giftedness of our child does not conform to our dream. The macho dad has a violin-playing, ballet-loving son. The artsy-craftsy homemaker's daughter is a radical feminist. We look at some families and cringe at God's sense of humor.

Dreams may help sustain us during the tough times. However, when our dreams conflict with reality, they can blind us to the Spirit's gifts within our child. As a father who is a biblical scholar is fond of saying, "God forbids graven images of the Divine. We parents should do like-wise—our children are not to be images of us."

Children are not to become clones of parents, neither are they to be the fulfillment of our personal dreams or goals. Children are to be the fulfillment of God's dreams for them. We cannot hold our children in bondage to our wishful daydreams, no matter how loving we consider those dream-bonds.

But relinquishing our dreams can be extremely pain-ful. To dream of being united with our child and that child's family in a close relationship is a most worthy dream. Many parents do enjoy such relationships, but not all.

Affirming Love and Faith

At times we may feel caught up in a whirlwind, com-pletely at the mercy of our family and outside events. We have control over nothing!

But that's an illusion. While there are many areas of life over which we have no authority or influence, we do have control over our reactions to these events.

No matter how intimidating the present whirlwind, we can choose to immerse ourselves in positive thoughts, affirming love and faith. No matter how forceful that whirlwind, we can choose to think only good thoughts, affirming confidence in our abilities and in the goodwill and giftedness of others. No matter how vigorous that whirlwind, we can choose to pray positive prayers, affirming trust in God's mercy and presence and guidance. God is with us in the whirlwind.

When we are most distracted and needful, using affirmations or mantras can be helpful. Any short saying, prayer, Scripture text, ejaculation, mantra, can be used as an affirmation. The tone of an affirmation is positive; it affirms what we desire—not as something missing but as something already present. We are thanking God now for granting to us that which we seek. We are affirming our confidence in God's presence, mercy, love. When used often and consistently, affirmations can restore our faith, strengthen our hope, bring peace of mind, change attitudes, reestablish relationships.

Affirmations

Mercy, peace, and love are mine in abundance. (Based on 2 John 1:3)

God is with me and with my child. We cannot go where God is not.

Today I am at peace.

My mourning is turned into joy; my sorrow into gladness.
(Based on Jeremiah 31:13)

I rejoice and give thanks in all circumstances.
(Based on 1 Thessalonians 5:16-18)

The LORD is my light and my salvation; whom shall I fear?
(Psalm 27:1)

The Lord of peace gives me peace at all times in all ways.
(Based on 2 Thessalonians 3:16)

The God of hope fills me with all joy and peace in believing,
so that I abound in hope by the power of the Holy Spirit.
(Based on Romans 15:13)

To Ponder

- *What is the most difficult aspect of parenting for me to surrender? How does God's love help me in this phase of parenting?*

- *What have been my dreams for my child? What are my child's dreams? What might God's dreams be for us?*

- *What is my greatest need today? What affirmation would be most helpful to me?*

Sustaining and Nurturing

The terms *religion* and *spirituality* are not synonymous; some cynics even consider them contradictory!

The main purpose of religion is to help us develop a relationship with the Divine. Spirituality is that relationship with the Divine. Phrased another way, our religion sustains and nourishes our spirituality.

Being "religious" usually means involvement in an institutional denomination and performing the accepted practices of that organization. Being "spiritual" usually means seeking a deeper relationship with the Divine—however that term is understood. This quest may be independent of any organized religion. For example, the Twelve-Step Programs, such as AA, have a deeply spiritual element, but are not connected to any religion.

The popularity of spirituality continues to grow as people discover that spirituality feeds their souls and empowers them, brings meaning to life, offers a needed inner connectedness and assists in answering the basic questions of human existence. It is what we yearn for, deep within us, as human beings. We desire to love and be loved, we desire wholeness, we desire to know more deeply whatever is true for us. The Second Vatican Council stated that we all hunger for an *experience* of God. It is this experience of God that is the goal of the spiritual quest.

Another reason for spirituality's popularity is our increasing awareness of the shortcomings of organized religions. The young—and the not-so-young—look at religion and see organizations that are into control and authority, are rigid and self-serving. Many people have a hard time accepting the positions of some churches concerning women or gays or the divorced, birth control or capital punishment or abortion, population and the environment, liberation of the oppressed, ways of achieving world peace. Others have been deeply hurt or alienated by the actions of the institutional church or its representatives. Still others note the shortcomings of some religious leaders: their hypocrisy or concern about money, their desire for prestige, or their lack of compassion and spirituality.

▶ Seek the LORD and his strength,
  seek his presence continually.
  (1 Chronicles 16:11)

▶ Now the Lord is the Spirit, and where the Spirit of
  the Lord is, there is freedom. (2 Corinthians 3:17)

Often, our honest answer to these criticisms must be "You are correct!" Religious organizations, composed of human beings, do reflect human failings. While many of us are able to look beyond the human limitations and benefit from organized religion, others, sometimes including our kids, find that to be exceedingly challenging.

When our adult children complain that they do not find a home in our own parish, that the liturgy does not speak to them and is not empowering or joyful, we must listen carefully to what they say. Are they speaking religiously? Or spiritually? Are they rejecting the Catholic Church or rejecting the church as it exists in that particular church community?

This distinction is important because often our kids are on a spiritual quest, seeking spirituality, talking about spirituality, and we may miss the obvious because our thinking and vocabulary are locked into the specifics of one religion or one parish. They may be seeking for themselves what we have already found that satisfies our own needs.

Today, there is much variation in church communities. Not all Catholic parishes are faith-filled representations of the gospel-in-action. Some, unfortunately, are oppressive and life-draining, offering little spiritual nourishment; others are vibrant and life-giving, made up of people who empower one another compassionately and graciously.

A growing number of parishes have wonderfully welcoming programs designed especially for alienated Catholics, or others who have serious disagreements with what they perceive as Catholicism. These hospitable parishes offer a safe place for people to question, express their doubts and continue their search free of pressure. Other parish communities have undertaken missions to be especially welcoming to gays and lesbians or to the divorced or single parents. Still others focus on social justice issues and working with the oppressed. Some offer more opportunities for lay participation. We can and should encourage our children to search out faith communities where they can be accepted, fed and nourished.

This hunger for spirituality exists in all of us, though it may be expressed and satisfied differently. To be truly whole spiritually, some people are directed by the Holy Spirit to go to a place different from their place of nurture to find God. When this happens, we parents are to honor that call by respecting what our child regards as holy, though it may be different from what we regard as holy. We can communicate with our child using language that is not specifically Catholic but spiritual, for the church is not an institution but the People of God.

▶ Though my Catholic faith is important to me, I know that once our kids reach majority, they have their rights. My hope is that they choose to have a spiritual life. (A parent)

▶ We parents love stability; we hope that parenting will be a stroll on a smooth firm path. But reality is "canoe stability." We rock in the waves—sometimes rather wildly— but we do avoid swamping. (A parent and canoeist)

Handing On the Faith

We are called to hand on our faith to our children. This means we can teach a belief-system and incorporate religious traditions into family life. While we hand on to our child how to name the holy as we know and experience it, the invitation to respond comes from God: It is grace. And in all instances of handing on, whether of intangibles like faith or something concrete like a book, there comes a moment when the person to whom it is handed must accept it. We can only offer our faith to others; we cannot accept it for anyone else, including our adult child.

▶ Being a Methodist minister meant our whole family was involved in church and social justice issues. Now one daughter is married and her family never goes to church. However, she is quite involved in helping others and I do believe that is her calling now. But I still wish it were different! (A pastor and parent)

▶ My nephew became a Buddhist. He lives a compassionate, meditative life. Unfortunately, my brother, his father, cannot recognize the good in his son's spiritual way. That young man lives a holier life than most Catholics I know! (A parent)

▶ We can take care of the garden but we don't make the plants grow. (A parent who is also a gardener and spiritual director)

Since each of us is a unique individual, we respond in our own way to what has been handed to us. Our child has his or her own unique way of processing what we have taught. Throughout our many years of parenting we have taught love of God, we have lived concern for neighbor. However, in our children this love and concern may be evidenced in different ways. We know many generous and accepting people, people whose lives embody the gospel message of love, yet who claim no formal religion. When our adult children say they have no religion, we note the goodness and spirituality in their lives, remembering that faith is broader than religion.

[W]hat does the LORD require of you but to do justice, and to love kindness, and to walk humbly with your God? (Micah 6:8)

Our Catholic tradition teaches that faith is a gift from God. Who of us can predict or understand God's ways or gifts or graces? The gift that our child receives may be what we desire: a faith-filled call to Catholicism. Or it may be an equally faith-filled call to Judaism or Islam or Baha'i, to Hinduism or Lutheranism or Native American spirituality. Our child may receive a call to be a seeker or a doubter. Such a call may be a temporary one during a period of questioning. It may be an act of rebellion while our child tries to determine who he is or what she wants in life. Or it may be a permanent one. We can hand on the faith, but our children may choose a different path. God's ways are mysterious. While we would always bear witness to our own faith and give reasons for our position, we must trust that our children are in the hands of God.

The Catholic Church does not reject anything that is true and holy in any of these religions and, in fact, looks upon them with sincere respect. Even though they differ from us, their ways of life and doctrines often reflect the truth that we all seek. The Church, of course, continues to proclaim Christ as "the way, the truth, and the life," but we also exhort all our members to be prudent and loving and open to dialogue with others. We urge Christians to defend and promote the spiritual and moral benefits found among other world religions, including the values found in their cultures. (*Nostra Aetate* ["Declaration on the Relationship of the Church to Non-Christian Religions"], from Bill Huebsch, *Vatican II in Plain English: The Decrees and Declarations, Book 3*, pp. 88-89)

Searching for Truth

The Quakers have a wise saying: "Each person has a piece of the Truth." This is one of the principles that enable the Quakers to find peaceful resolutions to conflict and to arrive at decisions based upon consensus, both on the local level and nationally.

Each of us—including our child—has a piece of the Truth. Recognizing this can help us maintain respect for our child's decisions. It can aid us in achieving consensus and at arriving at a peaceful resolution to conflict on the personal level.

Each religion also has a piece of the Truth. As Catholics, we are grateful for the truths God has preserved in the church down through the ages. However, we also recognize truths in other religions. Sometimes they help us better appreciate the truths we have. Sometimes they help us discover truths that we have neglected, forgotten or even distorted. We Catholics have given up the arrogant claim that only we have the road to salvation! While the Catholic tradition is our chosen way, we do recognize that there are many and varied paths to God.

An individual's search for his or her own truth can lead in diverse directions and include paths of serious doubting. And it is a common human trait that we learn best from our mistakes. Some of us make many mistakes before we discover what is true-for-us. For the lovers of the searcher, watching this quest can be painful.

During the process of growing up, the young ask themselves, Who am I? In attempting to answer that most individual question, the young begin by looking at their relationships with parents and family, at their heritage and culture, religion and politics and every other aspect of their lives. How am I similar to my parents? How am I different from my parents?—these questions are asked often, in ways both circumspect and confrontational.

Honestly searching for answers can be a lifelong task, but a necessary one, as we continue to learn of ourselves. Our quest leads us to claim or refuse attitudes, lifestyles, belief-systems, values and the rest of the legacy passed down to us by family and culture and religion. Each of us searches for understanding of what it means to be human, of what is the purpose of life. We are looking for our piece of the Truth based upon our experiences. We are developing an informed conscience. We are establishing our own relationship with the Divine.

▶ For me, a favorite and consoling quote is from Dostoyevsky: "True faith is forged in the crucible of doubt." (A parent)

▶ At first, it was very hard when my daughter married into another faith. But she and her husband are active in their church and my grandkids' bible study programs are better than any Catholic ones I've seen. Yet the pain of disappointment is still there. (A parent)

Thus, actions that we parents observe as negative may be elemental steps in our child's maturity. As one parent and spiritual director often counsels, "To question is healthy!" However, this questioning may result in a real test of parental faith as we are called to recognize that God's plan for our child may not be identical to ours.

Our children need to evaluate the messages handed on to them, so that eventually they can name and claim the sacred in their own lives. The so-called "crisis of faith" is a normal stage of the maturation process as they ask of themselves, Who is my God? What is my spiritual journey?

For our adult child not to attend church can be that individual's take-charge decision; it may not be a loss of faith but a time of testing the truth of that person's own experience. Since most people do have some kind of faith—with or without institutional religion—we need to recognize and be respectful of our adult child's choices. If we validate our child's decision we leave the door open for communication and, just possibly, for return—if the Spirit so directs.

O the depth of the riches and wisdom and knowledge of God! How unsearchable are his judgments and how inscrutable his ways! (Romans 11:33)

We here at Vatican II urge everyone, therefore, especially those in education, to form women and men who love true freedom: people coming to their own decision, using their own judgment, following the light of truth, being responsible seekers of goodness, and cooperating with others toward that end. True freedom, then, results in people who act with greater responsibility in fulfilling their obligations to the community. (*Dignitatis Humanae*, from Bill Huebsch, *Vatican II in Plain English: The Decrees and Declarations, Book 3,* p. 78)

To Ponder

- *How do I distinguish between religion and spirituality? Which is more important to me? Which is more important to my child?*

- *What aspects of religion or spirituality has my child accepted? Rejected? What aspects of religion or spirituality that were handed on to me have I accepted? Rejected?*

- *What are the core beliefs that I myself have deliberately and consciously chosen concerning family? Religion? Spirituality?*

Loving Our Children

No matter how much we parents love our children, God loves them more. No matter how much we have invested in our children, God has invested more. No matter how much we desire the well-being of our children, God desires it even more.

The love of God surrounds us all—parents and children. God is there to sustain us in difficulty, direct us in confusion, calm us in anxiety, comfort us in sorrow, rejoice with us in joy. God will not keep us from trials but is with us in those trials. God will not remove all cause for weeping but is there to weep with us. We can all say with confidence, "God is in this experience!"

So much has been written and sung and preached about love that the words seem glib and, when we are in crisis, may not reach our hearts. We crave the full and personal reassurance of God's love for us and for our child. We need to get in touch with our past experiences of God's love.

Once more we read and say aloud the words: the love of God is always here. Despite our own deafness and blindness and infidelity, God is always here. Despite the apparent deafness and blindness and infidelity of our child, God is always here, for God is love, passionate and inclusive love, radical love.

▶ When a parent comes to me with concerns about an adult child, I ask, "Do you love your child?" Invariably the answer is "Of course!" My response is "Do you think God loves that child less?" (A spiritual director)

▶ We are all addicted to something—work, sports, prestige, sex, hobbies, authority, substances. Why not be addicted to loving? Bring love everywhere to everyone! (A pastor)

God's view of us is penetratingly clear-sighted. God sees our failings, our limitations, our sins. However, God always looks at us with mercy, focusing on our intentions and efforts through our scars and pain. God sees perceptively, always looking beyond the present to what can be. God even sees love within us when we are not aware of its existence.

What an awesome power is love! All who love have that power—a power not based upon control or force or limitation. The power of love awakens the dormant potential that lies within the one loved. Love, being of God, is life-giving, nurturing, empowering of the other. Love is hospitable and welcoming, and love is freeing.

Love allows the one loved to be gloriously the person God created in love. And so we lean into God's love for healing, for strength, for love to give to our child.

> [F]or the LORD does not see as mortals see; they look on the outward appearance, but the LORD looks on the heart. (1 Samuel 16:7)

In this phase of parenthood—the parenting of an adult child—our call is not to judge, but to love abundantly without conditions. As one spiritual director and parent advises, "Love—no matter what!"

And so, despite the heartbreak and disappointments, we say to our child, as God says to us all, "I love you and I accept you." We say those words aloud to our child often, for all of us never outgrow the need and desire to be loved.

Believing in the Paschal Mystery

One of our basic beliefs is the paschal mystery, the death and resurrection of Christ. We affirm this belief at every liturgy: "Christ has died, Christ is risen, Christ will come again."

But this cycle of death and resurrection into new life occurs for each of us in countless ways. Our lives are a series of changes in which we say goodbye to one phase as we enter a new one. Some of these passages are gradual and gentle; others are distressingly painful, as God works slowly and anonymously in our lives. We leave our old home for a different one. We graduate from one school to enter the next. We leave one job to begin another. We leave the single state to enter marriage. We move from the parent/child relationship to an adult/adult relationship. We watch a problem transform into an opportunity for growth. We force old dreams to die to make room for new ones.

Each death and new life event comes at a cost. Often there is separation anxiety and fear, a feeling of stepping out into an abyss. There may be "tomb time"—when we seem to wait in vain and need to recall Mary's faithfulness, which continued even after the crucifixion.

Perhaps our vigil will end with a glorious announcement: "He is risen!" More often it will slowly conclude as the new life, new relationship, comes into being at an achingly gradual pace. But it does come.

Our belief in the paschal mystery sustains us in our belief in our child.

▶ God plants roses in ashes.
  (A Lutheran pastor and parent)

▶ If you believe in an all-loving God, then no matter what your adult child is doing now, all is not yet over—the fat lady hasn't sung! (A parent)

[W]e walk by faith, not by sight.
(2 Corinthians 5:7)

To Ponder

- *What does my love for my child teach me about God's love for me? What does God's love for me teach me about God's love for my child?*

- *What might Mary have experienced during "tomb time"? What are some examples of the paschal mystery in my life? When have I felt loss that has been followed by unexpected good?*

Talking and Listening

As parents of a newborn, we did the talking and our baby cried; now it is our adult child who does the talking while we may feel like weeping.

When our child turns away from the church, are we able to listen without passing judgment? Are we certain that our child is, in truth, rejecting the church's teachings? Many items of faith and ethics remain in discussion mode. Some things are more important than others, and it is possible to disagree with the prevailing thought and remain a faithful, practicing Catholic. Are we knowledgeable about these matters?

Or, when our son commits to a lifestyle foreign to us, can we maintain a relationship? When our daughter enters a marriage that we regard as disastrous, are we still able to affirm her? And, can we do all these things and still maintain our own integrity?

Communication during crisis is often difficult. If dialogue is still possible, if an honest exchange of ideas and emotions is achievable, then we are indeed blessed. If we can give our perspective with a gentle touch, with loving-kindness and even with a bit of humor, it is a special grace.

It can be helpful to attempt to view our child's life through his or her experiences, which are very different from our own. We can try to leave ourselves behind and envision our child being held by our compassionate Creator while we turn to the God-within, the Holy Spirit, to guide us in our words. But parental influence is still limited! Just as our parents, if they are still living, can only offer us advice, so we no longer have the right to try to force our child's actions. A common parental shortcoming: our children are always older than we realize.

▶ I still have to remind myself: my child is now an adult. I can't make him do anything! (A parent and spiritual director)

▶ We must maintain the relationship at all cost. Without that, we have nothing. (A parent)

▶ Once a year I invite our daughter to church, back to the faith in which she was nurtured. So far she has refused. But that's okay, for she is a seeker and I believe she is listening to God's call. (A parent and spiritual director)

▶ By every word and action and look and posture and gesture, communicate to your child "I love you, I accept you; I'm available and I want to listen!" (A pastor)

Although verbal communication may now be difficult, we know we have been communicating our values to our child for many years through example and action and oft-repeated words. Our child does remember—and will continue to remember—our familiar responses of wisdom, our deeds of love, our words of acceptance and affirmation and compassion, our faithfulness to our own call.

In our pain and frustration, it is easy to set conditions or deliver ultimatums, forgetting, in our emotion, that we are to act out of the abundance of God's love. God always gives us permission to come back, no matter what we have done. We cannot make a child feel that, having once chosen a different path, he or she can never return. God sometimes leads us, or our child, along back roads. And so, at appropriate times, we offer invitations to our child to return to the family, the church, the community.

Now may not be the time for words. As many parents can attest, harangues don't work! Lectures are ignored. Criticism, no matter how constructive, may prove counterproductive. As we learn in the story of Saint Francis, he said, "Preach always, and, when necessary, use words." This may be the time for preaching without words.

Changes in people's lives often call for changes in practices and rituals. When traditions get in the way of furthering relationships and fostering unity, we should not hesitate to create new traditions. Every tradition had a first time. Some mixes of the family simply do not work and, as one mother observed, "Getting together to be miserable is foolish!"

Rituals need not be religious to have a profound effect upon belief or actions. Any word or custom, whether sacred, secular, hilarious or reverent, that fosters unity, that reminds us of our connectedness or communicates love, has value. Any word or custom or traditional food that reminds us we are family has value. Ritual is essential to both individuals and family for it adds to solidarity, offers stability, provides a common memory.

It is time to be creative!

Of course, we parents do have rights. We have the right—and duty—to let our child know how we believe and what we feel. We have the right—and duty—to tell our child of our concerns about potentially dangerous actions, about possible illegal activities, about the consequences of following her or his chosen path. But we say these things always from and with love.

And so, if on a rare occasion we feel called to confront our child, as the biblical prophets were called to confront their people, we do so cautiously. The usual response of people to prophets throughout the ages has been negative and sometimes violent. So we do our confrontation gently and delicately, lest we find ourselves the recipient of the harsh fate that is visited upon so many prophets!

► Then Jesus said to them, "Prophets are not without honor, except in their hometown, and among their own kin, and in their own house." (Mark 6:4)

► For everything there is a season, and a time for every matter under heaven... a time to keep silence, and a time to speak.... (Ecclesiastes 3:1,7)

► Let us then pursue what makes for peace and for mutual upbuilding. (Romans 14:19)

Defining Successful Parents

How do we define "success" in parenting?

From our parenthood's beginning, we were surrounded by others who offered—or imposed—standards: neighbors who persistently informed us when our baby's "firsts" should occur, the dentist who considered us failures when our kid had a cavity, the scout leader who regarded a spotless uniform as a necessity, the religious education teacher who considered punctuality the highest virtue, the teacher who held parents accountable for homework, the coach who noted if a parent missed a game.

With experience, we also became wary of bragging about our kids' achievements. The neighbor's son who had excelled in school became a workaholic with a neglected family. Our second cousin, who had a problem-free adolescence, became a middle-aged divorcee immersed in a series of affairs. The well-known local "Catholic," who attends Mass faithfully, is on the fringe of every questionable or shoddy activity in the city.

So, how do we define "success" in parenting?

We know that everything our child does is not our fault. If our self-worth is dependent upon each day's evaluation of our parental success, we lose our credibility as a benchmark for our child. When this happens we become unable to respond reliably to our child should he or she ever consider changing paths.

Our worth as a person is not dependent upon our child's accomplishments; our identity as a person is not dependent upon our "success" as a parent. We are of value, not because of our achievements or those of our child; we are of value because we are God's creatures, created in the image and likeness of God, totally loved by God. All else is secondary!

Parenting is the unveiling of the wonderful mystery of God's creation that has been entrusted to us; success becomes a matter known only to God. God notes our efforts that seem fruitless, our frustrations of not knowing what to do, our faithfulness in loving. God sees our own childhood scars, the pressures of culture, our fatigue as we age, the times we have sought support and were disappointed by family and friends and even church. God sees all this and continues to hold us in love. To God, we, and our child, are never failures!

▶ The nurse at our family doctor's office was very curt when I didn't know all the inoculations that each of our five kids received. I, on the other hand, felt remembering their names to be an accomplishment! (A parent)

▶ If we get so hooked into a situation that our parental self-esteem comes into jeopardy, the less apt it will be to be resolved. (A parent and spiritual director)

To Ponder

- *Under what circumstances do my child and I communicate best? What can I do to improve our communication?*

- *How have I experienced outside pressures in my parenting? What are ways in which I am a "success" as a parent? How does God regard me a "success"?*

Seeking Help

When our child was young and we were confronted with problems beyond our expertise, we did not hesitate to seek help from doctors, teachers, coaches, youth ministers, other parents. Although our child is now an adult we should not allow shyness or embarrassment or parental pride to prevent us from asking for assistance.

We owe it to our child and to ourselves to ascertain the facts about the path our child has chosen. Misinformation and half-truths will not help us in our relationship or our communication. We need credible sources for the facts: What is the truth about this lifestyle? What does the church teach about it? Is this a matter that is under discussion within the church? We need to remember that there are many areas of theology and ethics where people can disagree with current church teaching and still remain faithful Catholics.

The amount of written material available today is incredible—name a situation and someone has written a book about it. Though resources abound, some cautions are necessary. Statistics can become out-of-date. Not all religious writing, even recent "Catholic" writing, is in harmony with the Second Vatican Council. And, just because something is on the Internet or on TV does not mean it is current. For example, the *Catholic Encyclopedia* that is available on the Internet is the 1917 edition!

Besides written materials, information and support, both for us and for our child, are available through organizations, governmental agencies and private sources. Pastoral ministers, spiritual directors and counselors can help us or point us in the direction of those who can. Assistance is available through parish or diocesan resources, local, county or state agencies and an increasing number of volunteer and support organizations.

Unfortunately, there are occasions when an adult child goes far beyond acceptable boundaries, choosing paths that lead to self-destruction, or involve illegal activities, or are dangerous to the individual or others. Fortunately, even then there is help. There are resources that provide us parents with intervention assistance and experienced people ready to carry out such intervention. We should never let fear or parental pride or embarrassment keep us from seeking such assistance, for our love puts our child's welfare above all else.

► Therefore encourage one another and build up each other.
(1 Thessalonians 5:11)

► "For nothing will be impossible with God." (Luke 1:37)

Caring for Ourselves

Despite the turmoil in our lives we still have a responsibility to care for ourselves. Self-care has high priority on our to-do list and is planned into every day.

- **We forgive ourselves**. No matter how many mistakes we now think we may have made in the past, we know we did the best we could at the time.

- **We acknowledge our psychological pain, our loss of dreams, our frustrations**. This is today's reality; now we gently prepare to move forward.

- **We don't allow grief or frustration to dominate other relationships.** We tend our other relationships with care.

- **We use wisely God's many gifts to us; we are good stewards.** No matter how trying the present, we do not waste our lives!

- **We remember to rest, to eat properly, to relax, to be with friends, to pray.** We treat ourselves occasionally to a massage, a day away, a ballgame, an evening at the theater.

- **We involve community.** Others can do what we cannot. Others can help us when we are in need. Others can help our child. Others can pray for us when we are unable to pray. Community is the beginning of the reign of God.

- **We focus on the positive aspects of our lives: our relationships, our faith, our family, our health, our country, our many blessings.**

- **We remain open to change.** Though we may fear the unknown, we affirm that God is always with us and will accompany us into the future.

► Do you not know that you are God's temple and that God's Spirit dwells in you?... God's temple is holy, and you are that temple. (1 Corinthians 3:16-17)

► "Come to me, all you that are weary and are carrying heavy burdens, and I will give you rest. Take my yoke upon you, and learn from me; for I am gentle and humble in heart, and you will find rest for your souls. For my yoke is easy, and my burden is light." (Matthew 11:28-30)

Praying for Peace of Mind

The situation can become so acute that we wonder at our own survival. Yet, not only can we survive, we can achieve peace of mind!

Peace of mind does not depend on outside circumstances; it does not remain elusive until we have everything we desire. Inner peace is not a state only for good times, but is achievable in difficult times. When we have inner peace we can respond to both good fortune and difficulties from a position of equanimity.

Peace of mind is an inward state of freedom from fear and the absence of hate; peace of mind allows us to give ourselves in love.

"God is in this experience!" We know, deep within every cell of our body, that God is with us. We feel God's love surrounding us. We experience a full realization that God is weeping with us. We touch God's tears even as we weep.

We pray that all of us be open to God's love and to the whisperings of the Holy Spirit.

DAILY MEDITATION

I envision, with compassion, my adult child.
I imagine my son/daughter embraced by God.
I imagine being united with my child in God's love.

A PARENT'S PRAYER

Creator God of all,
let me accept my child as you do,
let me listen to my child as you do,
let me love my child as you love my child.

To Ponder

- *If people in need do not seek help they deprive others of the opportunity to help. Who can I provide with such an opportunity?*

- *Which of the self-care mind-sets or activities in the "Caring for Ourselves" section would be most beneficial for me today? How can I enter into the activity or mind-set in a gentle manner?*

Summing Up

- We continue, always, to offer our child love—love that reflects God's unconditional love for us all.

- We maintain communication by focusing on areas of agreement and rituals that unite, always remembering that silence and listening are important elements of communication.

- We continue to pray and to parent by example, for to our child we embody the beliefs we profess.

- We dedicate ourselves to letting go of the negative emotions of guilt, shame, embarrassment, anger—we treat ourselves gently and lovingly.

- We let go of old dreams and old relationship habits, for they have served their purpose and it is time for new ones.

- We let go of our adult child, confidently placing our child in the embrace of a most loving God.

- We accept our adult offspring in the fullness of being. We accept limitations as well as talents. We accept personality traits, including those that are not of our choosing. We accept our child's path, for the Holy Spirit guides us all. We accept ourselves and our own paths.

- We remain open to the wisdom and guidance of the Holy Spirit, through whose direction the reign of God becomes reality.

We know that all things work together for good for those who love God....
(Romans 8:28)